From Loss to Enlightenment

Corinne Beth Gravenese

BALBOA.
PRESS
A DIVISION OF HAY HOUSE

Balboa Press books may be ordered through booksellers or by contacting:

Balboa Press
A Division of Hay House
1663 Liberty Drive
Bloomington, IN 47403
www.balboapress.com
1-(877) 407-4847

Because of the dynamic nature of the Internet, any web addresses or links contained in this book may have changed since publication and may no longer be valid. The views expressed in this work are solely those of the author and do not necessarily reflect the views of the publisher, and the publisher hereby disclaims any responsibility for them.

The author of this book does not dispense medical advice or prescribe the use of any technique as a form of treatment for physical, emotional, or medical problems without the advice of a physician, either directly or indirectly. The intent of the author is only to offer information of a general nature to help you in your quest for emotional and spiritual well-being. In the event you use any of the information in this book for yourself, which is your constitutional right, the author and the publisher assume no responsibility for your actions.

Any people depicted in stock imagery provided by Thinkstock are models, and such images are being used for illustrative purposes only. Certain stock imagery © Thinkstock.

ISBN: 978-1-4525-3421-3 (sc)
ISBN: 978-1-4525-3423-7 (hc)
ISBN: 978-1-4525-3422-0 (e)

Library of Congress Control Number: 2011905966

Printed in the United States of America

Balboa Press rev. date: 5/19/2011

Contents

Preface

I began writing this book while suffering the deep pain from the experience of losing my daughter. Though I was broken and shattered, there was a part of me that knew I had the ability to rise above the pain to see light again. As I began to see that light, I realized that the experience of losing my daughter held so much more for me than just pain. I started to trust in something I couldn't yet see but could *feel* on so many levels. I have confidence that you too will be lifted to a higher place, a place you have never been to before. I invite you into a world filled with hope where your spirit will be renewed and you will find a connection to your loved one that's beyond even your greatest expectations. Together, let's journey back to the light ...

The Beginning of the End

I found myself lying on the exam table at my OBGYN's office. When the doctor came around by my side after the exam, I had no idea how my world was about to change. She had a tender look in her eyes as she told me what no mother ever wants to hear in her fifth month of pregnancy. "Corinne, you're two centimeters dilated and your sac is bulging." I had a sinking feeling and couldn't help but cry. I had three healthy pregnancies before, and I knew the seriousness of this situation. *How can this be happening to me? I don't have these problems during pregnancy. I have full-term, fairly large babies at 37–38 weeks.* This was the beginning of the end—or as I was to find out, the beginning of the most life-changing experience I have ever had.

The next thing I knew, I was being transferred to a stretcher and sent to the hospital. On the way, I was shaking uncontrollably, tears rolling down my face, trying desperately to get in touch with my husband. There was no answer. Of all the times I ever needed him, it was now—and he wasn't there to answer my call. I needed someone to be by my side through this ... I just couldn't do it alone. My next call was to Amy. She was one of my best friends, and we shared our children's birth experiences with each other. She answered right away, and I could barely get the words out. "I'm on my way to the hospital. I may be losing the baby." She immediately got into her car and headed straight to the hospital. Even though the ambulance ride took only ten minutes, it felt like hours. I wanted so badly to be with someone close to me; I felt so alone. I needed a hand to hold, someone to tell me it was going to be okay.

Amy arrived shortly after the ambulance brought me into the ER. In my very brief visit to the ER, I was able to get a hold of my mother and my other best friend Colleen. They too were shocked to hear the news and immediately began making their way to the hospital. Amy held my hand the entire way to the maternity unit of the hospital. It meant so much to me that she was there with me—someone I loved and who I knew loved me. She was there by my side in my darkest hour.

After I arrived in my room (a room you're put in to deliver), there were many nurses hooking me up to monitors and IVs. The next thing I knew, my bed was placed in an inverted position. I was basically standing on my head. We had to do that in order to put the baby back up into its proper place. The hope was to get the baby back up in, high enough to give my cervix a stitch—or cerclage—in order to hold the baby up in there. At that point, I was not ready to accept anything other than, *it's going to ok*ay. I was confident that the doctors were going to get everything back to the way it needed to be in order for my baby to stay in long enough to be delivered normally.

My mother finally arrived at the hospital, she hugged me and we cried together. She had lost two children, a son and a daughter in two separate car accidents. This was a tender nerve for her, to watch as her daughter suffered with the loss of her own child. It brought back a lot of difficult memories for my mother. She just wanted to make everything okay for me so that I wouldn't have to hurt the way she did. Unfortunately, this situation was completely out of her control—and all of ours for that matter.

When my husband finally arrived at the hospital, he really had no idea of what was going on. This was a very unexpected event that had abruptly unfolded. After the situation was explained to him, that's when I really lost it. I cried so hard to him. I just wanted our baby to be okay. He was so strong. Patrick had been in the Marine Corp and had seen many tragic events unfold right in front of his eyes, but this was different. This was his own child. It was a part of him that was at stake. Patrick and I share a very special kind of love—a love that some call *soul love*. When we first met, we had an instant connection and felt as if we had been together before this lifetime. From the very beginning, my relationship with him was different from any other relationship I had ever had. There in the hospital, his embrace meant everything to me. He whispered softly in my ear, "It's going to be okay."

I somehow knew this situation was not going to be okay though. It was a gut feeling, a deep inner knowing. Yet I was still determined to stay optimistic. *This is my daughter, my child, my heart and soul growing inside me. I need her to make it.*

The News

*T*he very next day, they were going to check to see if the baby's sac had receded enough to put in my stitch. My husband had just started a new job and wasn't able to stay with me at the hospital that day. My dear friend Colleen, who was more like a sister, was there by my side through the entire process. She stayed with me as they wheeled me down to the room that they would be doing my exam in. I was so nervous, scared of the unknown. This was the deciding factor between life and death. It's interesting what you remember in times of crisis; I can still clearly recall what the nurses talked about as they wheeled me down the hall. They were chatting about what a beautiful ring I was wearing. I couldn't help but think about how unimportant any ring or material object was; those things meant nothing to me! I just wanted to hear the doctor say that everything was okay and we could go ahead with the stitch.

It was a feeling like no other when he said, "I'm sorry, but your sac does have a leak, and there's nothing that I can do."

What? This cannot be! "Well what can we do about this?" I questioned. "There's got to be something we can do!" He informed me that the only thing I could do was go home and wait for the baby to come. I was two weeks shy of the almighty twenty-four weeks that I needed to be in order for the baby to have a fighting chance. So just go home and wait for her to come naturally? It was very simple to him, as it is for most doctors in this situation; this is something that they see all the time. If you're not at least twenty-four weeks into your pregnancy, your baby simply cannot live. The baby is considered not viable up until that point. Even so, I couldn't believe how callus and cold the doctor was. This was *my* baby, my daughter, who was perfect in every way. *She can't come yet.* I cried harder than I had ever cried in all of my life at that moment. Nothing can prepare a mother for this kind of heartache—not even watching your own mother suffer through the loss of her two children.

Maybe I'll wake up and this will all be a part of a really bad dream, I thought as they wheeled me back to my room. I had to wait, and as I waited, I cried until my mother, Patrick, and his parents arrived. The nurses had unhooked me from all of the monitors. They let me sit up in bed. Get up and walk around. They had given up hope. We were all shocked at how quickly the doctors and hospital staff had given up. When Patrick, his parents, and my mother arrived, there were lots of questions. *What should I do? Where do we go from here? Another hospital? Get a second opinion? Should we at least go to a hospital that's capable of taking care of a premature baby?* That night, we decided to go to another hospital and get a second opinion. By the next morning, I had a team of doctors working with us to determine if in fact my sac was torn and how to proceed from there. I wish I could say they had a different diagnosis, but they only confirmed the situation. In addition, I had started to develop an infection from my cervix being dilated, a common occurrence in this type of situation. I had been checked and rechecked by a staff of doctors that were some of the best in the country, and there was nothing any of them could do. I was going to deliver this baby. My body had started labor.

I had my husband, my sister, Debbie, and my two best friends with me during this process. Although I would have liked for my boys—who were seven, eleven, and fifteen at the time—to be a part of this delivery, they were over an hour away, and looking back, it was probably for the best that they didn't have to see their mother suffering so. How could I be there for them when I could barely get myself through this? I felt so much guilt. I was failing my daughter. I was failing my husband. It just wasn't fair that she wouldn't be able to survive outside of my womb. As much as modern technology has made advancements in medicine, they have yet to replicate the womb of a mother, and no matter which doctor we talked to, they all had the same answer. You have to be at least twenty-four weeks for the baby to make it—if there's any chance at all. As strange as it may sound, I felt as though this was part of a bigger plan. I was twenty-two weeks along, and on some level I felt that if she was meant to make it, this would have happened two weeks later. But the looming question was, *why?* Why should anyone suffer so?

Our daughter was born 1 pound 2 ounces and 12 inches long. She was so little but so full of unconditional love—the kind of love that people somehow seem to lose after living life for twenty, thirty, or more years. She was a reminder of how magical unconditional love is and how that is who we *all* truly are! We come from a place of unconditional love yet live in such contrast to that. We all got to hold her and smell the sweet baby smell of her little head. We took pictures and had her baptized. We all cried. Then after two hours, her heartbeat left her body and her love returned to the place from which it came. My sister and friends left us alone to be with our daughter, Norah Lee Gravenese.

My husband and I lay in the bed holding our daughter. This was my husband's first child; I had three boys previously. I hated the fact that this was Patrick's first child and she came and left so quickly. Not one part of any of this seemed fair. Although this was not my first but my fourth, it was my first girl, the daughter I had so longed for. This had not been the birth experience we had both been dreaming of, not even close. One thing we did know was how much we loved each other—how he and I were one, and there was no separation. When couples go through something traumatic, such as losing a child, it will either bring them closer or push them apart. I needed Patrick like I needed air. Without him, I may have died inside that day. There would be many days ahead that I would just lie next to him while he was sleeping and press my lips on his forehead; it somehow connected me to her. He was my closest connection to our baby. She was just as much a part of him as she was me. This was clearly obvious looking at all of her different parts that resembled both of us. She had my nose and his mouth, my ears and his fingernails. She was our love and our hearts in one tiny body. Perfect in every way!

I had an ache in my heart that was so deep and painful, I didn't think I could ever be whole again. I was without any doubt smashed to smithereens. How does anyone ever recover from the loss of a child? How do you recover from losing something you love more deeply than anything else in the world? I didn't know how I would get through all of this, but I knew I would—I had to.

Coming Home

I was now part of the group of mothers that leaves the hospital without a baby in their arms. I was waiting in a wheel chair by the door with all of my bags, a stretched out belly, and no baby to take home with me. I had never known that feeling before. As I watch other mothers waiting for their rides with a brand-new baby to take home, I couldn't help but feel saddened by it. I now had a whole new understanding of mothers who have to leave the hospital with empty arms not only once but several times.

The ride home was tough. Patrick picked me up, and as we began our journey back to our house with our broken hearts, we realized how undone we both were. In fact, he drove the car down a one-way road without even realizing it. I cried most of the way home, not believing I would ever be able to stop crying. It was a long ride, almost an hour.

When we arrived, my father pulled in the driveway at the same time. He lived three hours away, so this was the first time I was seeing him since all of this had started to happen. I'll never forget how important it was to me that my Dad was there to hug me when I first got home. He was so sad; I had never seen him tear up like that before. He was the kind of man that usually showed little emotion. I knew he was hurt to the core watching me suffer through the pain of losing my baby. My oldest son was home, and the other two were with their father. I don't think my son knew what to say. Does anyone during times like this? He didn't get to hold her and feel her love himself, but he got to feel the essence of what she brought to all of us that did. Everyone there for the delivery was changed in so many ways. She touched all of our hearts. So little and so full of love.

Soon others began to show up. My Aunt Beth and my cousin Marissa came with food and lots of love and support. Looking back, it was all a big blur. When you suffer through something traumatic, it's difficult to remember things clearly. Many people called to send their condolences. It was all so nice and I wish I could remember more, but honestly I was quite out of it. For the next couple of weeks, my dear friends Amy and Colleen made sure that I had someone with me every day. They helped with the boys, they cleaned, they cooked, and they were right there if I needed anything.

I spent many days crying, longing to have my baby back. I knew there had to be a deeper meaning in all of this and that I just couldn't see it yet, but that didn't lessen the pain. I yearned for her back and felt so far from where she was. About three days after coming home, my breasts started to fill with milk. I never thought this would happen, but I did deliver a baby and that's part of the natural way of things. I always breastfed my children, so again I was hit with a horrible feeling of loss. How could this be fair—all this milk and no baby to feed?

For the first several weeks, there was no relief in store for me. My husband, however, was strong and continually tried to comfort me. He consistently promised me that it would be okay, but I just couldn't relate at all. He was my pillar of strength, and I knew deep down that I needed him to be in his positive mindset in order to help me get through all of this. He had completely and fully accepted the loss of our child and was prepared to just move forward. Truly, isn't that all anyone can do? Going back simply isn't an option. Reliving it over and over in your mind cannot change *any* of it. I knew he was right in his steadfast determination to keep moving forward, but I was resistant to letting go, somehow feeling as if that would be giving up on my daughter. Though we all know that makes no sense, in my grief I couldn't see that.

Is there any love deeper than that of a mother and child? Of course there are in fact mothers out there who are disconnected from their children, but they are few and far between. They are the ones who simply came here to be an incubator (if you will), to bring a life into the world. For me, motherhood has been such a profound experience. Starting motherhood at the sweet, young age of seventeen, I gave birth to my son, who is now fifteen. He completely changed the direction my life was going in at that time, and for that I know he was my savior. The day he was born, everything stopped being about my own self-destruction and became about caring for this bundle of love. He was something to love when I wasn't even sure how to love myself. I know without any doubt that our children are a mirror reflection of who we are. They will shine bright for you all the things that you're missing in yourself. For example, strength—if you're weak-minded, they'll completely take over, and you'll feel defeated over and over again. Now, the question remained: what did our daughter come to teach me?

The Awakening

*P*atrick and I had decided to take a trip to Tahiti the year prior to losing Norah, knowing there was something special in store for the two of us to share in this experience. Not only was it an amazing vacation, but it was also a part of an Abraham-Hicks seminar cruise. They are also called well-being cruises, and I strongly believe they keep you positive and on the leading edge of thought. We met two friends that I knew would be a very special part of our life. Nancy was one of those friends. She and I stayed in contact via e-mail, but it wasn't until this situation with our daughter, Norah, that we really connected. I remembered that Nancy had written a book after her husband had passed away and that it was about recovering after death, divorce, or separation. So I contacted Nancy soon after my loss, and she immediately sent me her book. It was exactly what I needed to help lift me enough to start to *feel* again.

Nancy and I continued to share e-mails back and forth, and I started to feel energized every time we connected. I was at a loss as to why this had all happened to me the way it did. She suggested that I go into a meditation and ask Norah to share with me the purpose of our experience together. Knowing that there was meaning behind Nancy's feeling for me to do this, I followed the suggestion. It may seem like an odd thing to do, but I needed answers. I needed to know what happened, why I lost Norah, and some of the reasons behind all of the pain and suffering.

This may seem like a difficult meditation to do. It may even seem weird, but I felt it was worth getting past all of that to feel the presence of someone so very close to you who has passed—as you'll soon see. Keep in mind that if you are in a lower vibration of energy (sorrow, sadness) you will not be able to connect to the higher vibration of where they now reside. Aware of that, I waited until it felt like the right time to do the mediation, a time when I was alone and in a place of clarity.

I started off by first asking her to be with me. I wanted to feel her love again. I recognized her energy as soon as I began feeling a connection to her; the love I felt wrapped around me was so familiar that I couldn't deny it was coming from her. I knew undoubtedly that this was Norah and we were now both in the same stream of energy. Next, I asked in my mind what it was like for her to be inside me. *Can you share what feelings and emotions I had been living with?* She began to show me the deep sadness that I had carried. She showed me all the fears and self-sabotaging thoughts that I was holding onto. I had no idea that I still hadn't let those things go, allowing them to dissolve into my past where they belonged. At the same time, I *did* remember feeling those things during the pregnancy, an inner sadness of some kind. She showed me that in order for me to go forward on my true path, I needed to, once and for all, let those parts of my past go. I needed to decide that I wouldn't continue for one more day to live my life in *fear*.

I remember thinking what a powerful teacher Norah was, and I knew that she would continue to be forevermore. I knew she would become my teacher of strength and that I could always look to her to show me the way. This was her way of letting me know that she would be there with me as I began to release all of these things one by one. She would be there to remind me of the greatness of the love of the universe and all the things I could delight in if I let go of my fears. She was saying, *Go on and live life fully because that's why we come here. Not to just sit back and let life take us over. We are here to be creators and lovers and livers of life!* Let's think about this. How many fears do we accumulate in a lifetime? How many things does this hold us back from doing? Why is it so many settle for the least when they can be having only the best? Why is life so dull and even hard at times when it could be full of captivating manifestations? Why should we settle for the life that our parents told us was realistic or possible? My daughter and I now shared an understanding that our lives would be a beautiful co-creative relationship from where she now resides in the non-physical, with me here in this earthly body. There is no age in the non-physical dimension. She is a part of all that is, and from that perspective, she is eternal, pure, positive energy. There is no beginning and no end. This was a very exciting revelation for me. It put purpose behind so much pain.   My husband had a saying from his time in the Marine Corp: *Pain is fear leaving the body.* I didn't fully understand the truth of that statement until I lost my daughter (physically speaking.) The pain I felt with the hit of such devastation was beyond words. The beautiful part in this was that the fear was lifting. Every day, I realized how trivial things that used to upset me and have me worried became a non-issue. Every heartache and every injury brings you to a place of "one less thing to hurt over," and you watch as fear dissolves itself from the body. You recognize that from here forward it must be about you and what *your* truth is—not that of others. You just can't be concerned about what others will think about you or fear for you. It is now a non-issue.

The magic is in turning your pain into the strength, drive, and determination to never again live your life in fear. When someone throws one (or more) of *their fears* your way, you say, "No thanks, that's your stuff." You can hold solidly and truly to who you have now become! Now that is a true awakening—to say, "I'm going to take the leap of faith because, hell, what is there to lose? Nothing can compare with the pain I just went through."

So for those of you reading this who have suffered through a loss, I would like to say, congratulations! You now have something that others will never have the opportunity to experience. You have been given a gift in all of this hurt and that is *in the strength you now possess.* Fear will never again take hold of you and rob you of the life that is truly meant for you. We are now deeply and eternally connected to those we have lost (physically). If you can wrap your head around this, it is profound. It is huge in terms of where you now stand! You are now joined with them in a place where *all* things are possible. If you allow yourself to be in a place of *connection* (higher vibration), you will live life to the fullest and will come to have a deep appreciation for life and all of its surroundings. You can and will live life like never before! You will be at the forefront of all creation and will enjoy the leading edge of going from thought to manifestations! Every hug and kiss you get from a child, friend, or loved one will be captured in a place of eternal appreciation. Doors will open for you that never had been before.

Why? Because *you lost the fear of losing.*

Fear (doubt) is the only thing that keeps you from the life that you having been asking for not only verbally but in every situation you are given by contrast. In this place of appreciation, you have tapped into this stream of energy that is life-giving. This is where you want to be if you want to feel *freedom*. Our lost loved ones are not lost at all; they are completely and fully with us in every way we can possibly think of and more.

We need to open our eyes to a new way of grieving. Why not completely and fully allow ourselves time to heal, mourn, and cry, and in the midst of all of this we become completely aware of how our lives are about to change for the better! You can do both! *You can feel the sadness and know at the very same time that this is about to bring you to a new life.* Now you have taken something that you would be resistant to and turned it into something you can embrace—the new life you are about to embark on. You will feel the ease in this action because you will have gone from resistance to allowance. That's the difference between paddling upstream against the current and paddling downstream with the current. **Feeling the sadness and allowing it**. Read this again and again until you get this. This is something that will change everything.

This can be applied to anything painful in life. We can suffer loss in many ways not just through the "death" experience. You can suffer loss through the ending to a relationship and find it to be almost unbearable and seemingly comparable to the devastation of loss through death. Some have lost their homes and felt the –hit- of loss as well. ANY of these scenarios can be applied to feeling "loss." The most important thing you can do is to *allow* the suffering. Try this for yourself and see how this can actually bring you to feel relief.

The Emotional
Roller Coaster

I cannot tell you that once you've made that amazing discovery you'll never have any more moments of sadness. There will be times when it will creep back up on you. It can happen when you see someone with what you lost, but it can also happen completely out of the blue. I will never forget the time when my husband and I had just had dinner at a restaurant and everything was perfectly fine—and the next thing I knew, I had burst into tears! Not just a normal cry but sobbing with big tears running down my face. As if we don't confuse men enough with our normal mood swings, my husband had absolutely no idea what had just happened. Nor did I for that matter. It seemed to have come out of nowhere. He kept asking me what happened, and I had no idea what to tell him. It was because nothing did just happen, except that at that particular moment in time, my body had to release some energetic sadness that I was still carrying around with me. Instead of being upset that it was happening, I embraced this as *healing* and knew that it would soon pass.

By allowing emotion to rise up within you without fighting it, you stop resistance. When you don't resist a negative emotion, it brings you to a higher place of healing and it does this fairly quickly. Try it and you'll see the difference. Allow the sadness and feel it fully. Know that it is part of your *human quality* and be grateful for the experience. In the act of doing this, you transmute pain into enlightenment. You experience your own miracle. We have many miracles that we experience in our lifetime, but they often go unnoticed. We expect them to be a catastrophic experience, but that's not always the case. When you start getting the hang of doing this, you begin to embrace the everyday hurts that we all encounter throughout our lives. You begin to feel enlightenment over and over again. You realize you've been given opportunities to rise above the mundane efforts of society and have reached a higher place, one of delight. There is no telling what will now come your way. Problems are no longer problems, only solutions and resolutions to life's situations.

The old ways are no longer working for us. We have seen many fall in the face of adversity, but now is the time to bring a different message, one of hope for a *new life* and a *new way*. When one perceives *loss*, it is truly only *perception* because there is no real loss. This is what we have created in our minds. We need to send a new message to those ready to hear this—that is, to awaken to the fact that we are connected and can never be separate from anyone or anything. Our minds are the *only* thing separating us from our loved ones that we call "passed," "dead," and "gone." They are no further from you than the day they were physically here! Our mind has created this as an illusion. When you open your mind to the infinite possibilities that this brings to you, you open a door to a higher platform, one in which anything and everything is possible! Your loved one is calling you into this life. They want you to see it from their vantage point. They want you to be where you are living in contrast, and at the same moment tap into the unlimited-ness of where they are! When you openly reach for them, you are sucked into this vortex of energy, and that energy is the one that creates worlds! Can anyone access this place? Yes. Do you have to lose a loved one to be there? No. Do you want this so much more than anyone who has not lost their loved one? Absolutely yes!

So what's stopping you from reaching out for them? What you've been taught? What your parents told you was truth? What your religion has taught you all these years? Really? Come on now. We can have so much more in life, and we continue to settle for so much less just because we've been taught limits. I will say to you, if this is what you are comfortable with for your life experience, then great. I wish you the best a mediocre life has to offer. But if you want to *live it* and I mean really *live it*, then open yourself up to this idea and new way of life. This may be so far stretched from where you are now, but that can change day by day by just staying open to this possibility. You have every right to continue to sulk in your sorrow for the rest of your days here in this physical body, or you can begin to live the high life (high in every sense of the word!) Every moment matters in this life, yet we often find ourselves just flailing around, being bounced all over the place because we have no idea what we're really here for. I can tell you, it's not what we've been conditioned to believe. Not even close! We are multifaceted beings with the power to do amazing things, and we need to access this energy within us.

This very moment can be the tipping point for a life change so huge that only those of the same energy will be able to keep up with you. There will be some who are left in the dust as they watch you amass the life most will only dream about! They will say, "What on earth has taken that person over? I want some of that! Sign me up, please." It will be just your very example that will inspire others to want to partake in the life you are now living. So will you rise to the occasion or falter with the rest? There's so much confusion amongst us when it comes to how to be and how to live. I think we've made this way too complicated and un-enjoyable!

My wish is for those who are ready to hear this message to viscerally feel all of these words and the energy I am projecting into them, to embrace it fully within themselves. Sit with it, allow it to resonate, ponder it, *feel* the words. The message is bigger than you even realize. Once you start this process, you will feel a new life brewing within you, a knowing that *all* things are about to shift and begin anew.

Here's to a New Life

As we begin to focus on this new life you are about to embark on, it's necessary for me to express the importance of a solid foundation. This foundation will prevent some of the setbacks and challenges that would undoubtedly come without it. When you begin to lay the structure for a magnificent building or home, if you don't use the proper material to ensure a solid foundation, you can lose everything! Since I didn't have a solid foundation, my life came crumbling down around me in every way imaginable. Had I built my life from the bottom up, and had I done so with "materials" that were of solid structure, then I wouldn't have needed this life-changing lesson to teach me the importance of having a solid foundation. It's critical to build your life on YOUR truth and not those of others. This is when you take what feels right to you and then you make that your life experience. This is when you decide to make the dream as big as you wish it to be and not settle for the little bits that others told you were all you could have in life. Through your solid foundation, you will find your truth, and that truth will set you free. *Free from what?* You may ask. Free from the enslavements of fear and all of its ugliness. Make a promise to yourself that from this day forward you will be a part of this *new life*, and then hold solidly to that promise.

Then it will be my promise to you that as you read these words that flow effortlessly from my fingertips, you will begin to heal. And as you heal, you elevate yourself to higher levels of energy, and as you move into these higher levels of energy, life will begin to captivate you. Soon you will look around and find yourself in awe of life itself. You will begin to see life pulsing in every living thing, big and small. You will see meaning in the seemingly meaningless. You will begin to have a zest for life and see through eyes of wonderment.

So let's celebrate the new life you're beginning at this very moment and embrace it fully. This is not going to be hard work; this is going to flow easily and effortlessly. This will now become who you are on every level. It is a transformation of self and all of the particles of life. If this all sounds good to you, then keep reading. If it doesn't, then stop reading. It's as simple as that.

From this point forward, you will do only the things that feel true to *you*. Everything will be about what feels best to *you*—not your partner, not your parent, not your pastor or your child, just *you*. This may sound simple, but believe me, it's not for most people because we're so hung up on making everyone else around us happy. This has been the way of life for years and years, and to change that is going to be easy only if you are 100 percent on board with this concept. You can't let your fear of what others will think hinder you or affect you in any way. Your life is yours to live, and there is no other person on this planet who can live it for you.

We have become so accustomed to the idea of letting other people's fears of what may happen influence our decisions. The first step is to simply recognize that this is the way it has been for a long time. Once you recognize it, you will see evidence over and over again of people around you allowing others' fears to influence them.

No one can make a better decision for you than you can—not if you're going forward without fear. There will be times when you question yourself and your ability to make the right decision, but those doubts don't have to hinder you for long. If you recognize them the instant they creep in, you can begin to make a change in your thinking. It's that simple. Just shift your thinking from one of fear to one of knowing that you will find the solutions you are asking for. In this asking, you create a powerful vortex around what you are wanting. This powerful vortex will lead you right into the perfect answer. Give it a try and see for yourself how perfectly this works. Ask the question. Be open to receiving the answer, and then in a little bit of time it will be answered for you.

Oftentimes in life, we need to take a leap of faith. We need to make a decision without knowing what the answer will be. For instance, imagine you've been asking for change in your life because you aren't happy with the way your relationship is going. It's no longer working for you, and it doesn't make you feel amazing like it should. So you take a leap of faith and say, *I'm going to end this thing that is no longer working for me. I don't know what's awaiting me, but I know it will be great because I'm trusting in something bigger than myself.* It's about closing a door with only the faith that you have within. This is when we get our biggest blessings—when we completely surrender without knowing what's next for us! It is in these moments that you will have the opportunity to witness a real-life miracle take place around you. Miracles are not a rare event that only "certain" people can experience. They are without a doubt an everyday occurrence, but often we are not in a place to appreciate what just happened right in front of us because we are so wrapped up in the "problems" around us. However, problems are not really problems, but *contrasts* we have come here to experience for our own expansion. If nothing ever went wrong, then there would be nothing to bring us to the conclusions of what we are wanting next. A new platform, so to speak. That new platform is now the jumping off place for other things. That's what expansion is, and *that* is what we came into this physical life to experience. It can be hard for us to see that when we are just looking at a situation as a "problem," but again, a shift in our thinking will begin to change that.

The most beautiful part of life is the ever-changing energy in us. Life's universal energy is always moving. When we feel stuck, we are not moving with the energy around us. That's when we become sick; our cells are at odds with each other because they're doing something different from what we are doing. They're always regenerating and becoming more, and if we're in a *standing still* or *standing against* pattern, then we're going to feel the discord. We're either moving with or moving against this ever-flowing energy, and you will know which you're doing by how you're feeling. Your emotions are your guide. If something feels bad to you, it's because you are resisting the direction that energy is moving toward. You don't necessarily have to be moving if you can just allow the energy to move itself—and believe me, it will. Allowing is really the key here.

Going through life on a softer, more joyful path is very much a possibility, even after a loss. I know this firsthand and am proof of this. We have been trained to suffer through "bad" situations, so we automatically do just that. However, you can break that pattern, starting today, right now. You can retrain your brain and begin a different way of life. When a "problem" or "loss" arises, you can become aware that something has just happened that's taken you off track from being the person you truly came here to be. Your thinking must shift in order for you to get back on track, to become again the joyful person that you really are. Until you do this, you will be continually fighting against yourself and feel very bad in doing it. It's no wonder there are so many diseases out there. How can anyone's body thrive in an environment that is so conflicted within itself?

Connecting to that Place of Wonderment

For those of you who have suffered through a loss, the following chapters will be of highest benefit to you. They will describe how powerful this connection to your loved one is for you here on this physical plane while your loved one is in the non-physical plane.

Since the beginning of time, there has always been a question of where we go after death. What is death and how would you define it? Everyone's answers vary greatly. In these pages, I will bring you to an understanding of death through my perspective and my personal experience. I was raised with the belief that, at the time of death, everything is gone and you become a "memory in God's mind." Then one day, he will wake you up in a paradise where all others who have died will be resurrected with you. This never made sense to me and never felt good to me. It took me about twenty-five years to be able to stand up and admit that to people who so deeply believe this as their truth. I knew I had to speak my truth if I were ever to be truly happy. Anytime you do anything for those around you instead of yourself, it feels so wrong that your body becomes miserable, sad, lonely, and even depressed.

The time came for me to say to everyone that I was done with the old beliefs and I was going to do what felt right to me from now on! To this day, my mother still cannot accept my belief about death—that there isn't any. She is so entrenched in what others told her was the truth. This is typical of religion. It keeps you scared, living in fear if you dare not to believe everything *they* say to be true. It amazes me to see this happen over and over again. People don't believe they have enough strength to rely on their own guidance system. Instead, they look to those around them to give them the answers, even when it feels wrong. Religions teach us to be so afraid of death so that they can continue to have power over us. Is there a way to know 100 percent for sure exactly what happens when we die? Not exactly. What we do have is the ability to access those who have already died, or even those who have had near-death experiences. Most of them say the same thing—what a wonderful feeling place they are in during this time. A common theme is that it's almost indescribable and so amazing to "see and feel the light."

When you have the opportunity to feel the presence of your transitioned loved one around you, then you will be able to share with others the depth of one's existence after "death." In order to feel our non-physical loved one, our energy must be a vibrational match to theirs. From where they are now, a part of All That Is, they are of a higher and lighter frequency. They are much more than we remember them to be because they have shed the body that held them from becoming one with source. Now they belong to an ever-flowing, unlimited in every way, stream of consciousness.

What is this stream of consciousness? It's the energy of source and what many call God; it is creation and creator all in one. From this energy force, we have been given all of creation. This is the power that creates worlds. This is who we all are prior to our entrance in this physical body, and this is also the energy force that keeps our hearts beating and our organs working. So when you hear the expression "we are all One," it's because we all flow from the same energy source. The only thing that separates us from who we truly are is the mind and its ability to disconnect from that which we call source. The mind is a very powerful instrument that keeps us separate from the beasts of the planet and all other living things. In our human form, we have been given this mind and body to experience the contrast. Contrast is what creates desire for more, for change and for expansion. Without it, our species would cease to exist. There would be no point in being here if we were to stay in sameness.

All things large and small have the ability to ask for change. As these things are asked, our very powerful non-physical staff answers and then holds those answers in escrow (if you will) until we line up our energy with the answer of these things. What is lining up energy? This means to be in a place where you are a match. How do you become a match? You hold firmly to what you have envisioned for yourself and remember at all times that these things are coming. In fact, not only are they coming, they are already here. That may sound confusing. If something is already here, you would see it with your eyes and experience it with physical touch, right? That's the point—bringing these creations into our minds/thoughts is what brings them into existence. You must first go there in your mind; they then become present in your experience.

Now this is so much better than it being physically present immediately because you can make changes along the way. You can mold this creation into exactly what you want it to be. If you get every detail ironed out before physical manifestation, through fine tuning it in your mind first, then you will be more than happy with your end-result manifestation. The clearer the details you create in your mind, the better the results will be.

Our loved ones that are now in this place of non-physical are wanting so much for us to get this. They want us to be able to create our life how we want it to be and stop settling for the same old mundane ways of our past. They want us to get excited about creating our future and see that things can be absolutely wonderful for us if we can just change our thinking. Think about what your loved one would say to you. I remember hearing a mother talk about her daughter after she was killed in a car accident. The woman said that in her mind she could hear her daughter saying, "Mom, you just got to live it." The mother had been stuck in a rut, in a funk, held down by the sadness of her daughter being gone. She wasn't really gone at all; she was just no longer in the body her mother once knew her to be in. Her daughter knew the importance of just living life for the time that you're here in this body. She didn't want her mother to waste one minute feeling bad—because there was nothing to feel bad for.

If we could only know how fabulous it is to be where our loved ones are, we would never have problems with death again. My daughter Norah came to me one day and said, "Mom, life is your playground." You got to get out there and have fun. That's what it's all about. We have this earth here as our platform, and we have so many different things to capture our interest and challenge our minds. This is supposed to be fun—not drudgery. If you're not going to create a wonderful life experience for yourself while you're here, then why be here? Have you ever seen the children in Africa with life-threatening diseases and how happy they are to be alive? They're sick and dying, and yet they still find happiness. Or here you can see children dying of cancer who have the biggest smiles and are the most wonderful teachers of just enjoying today. They enjoy what they have at this very moment because who knows what tomorrow can bring. It's a beautiful example of how you can find happiness in any situation. It's all about how you look at life.

Life gives you all of the things you expect it to. If you expect to be late, you will be late. If you expect to have problems, you will have problems. If you expect for things to work out easily, they will work out easily. Your thoughts are your most powerful creative forces. Understanding this makes you think twice about having negative thoughts, because you realize that those thoughts are going to create negative situations in your life. If every day you set the intention to make life your playground, then the universe will begin to yield this to you as your experience. You will begin to see the world as you have never seen it before. Then as you move forward with life, instead of against it, you will connect every day with your loved one that is now in the non-physical. You will become the energy match to them in their state of joy (bliss.) They are saturated in the energy of love and an awareness of the vastness of life. You will begin a co-creative experience with them. They will be so much more than what they were when they were here. When you ask for them to be with you and you are matched up to their energy, you will have a zest for life unlike any you've ever had before. The world will open up to you as if you've been given a new set of eyes. All of your experiences will be filled with a passion beyond belief. Your connection with them is your ticket to have this.

In the energy of the vortex you create with your loved one, you'll feel the fullness of life as they feel it from where they now reside. Once you get a taste of this in your experience, you'll never want to be without it again. You will be called back to this place over and over. The desire to feel in alignment with who you are truly meant to be will be so strong that your old feelings about life will no longer suit you. When we take this step, we take it fully and completely. We have a deep, inner knowing that we have come to a whole new platform, and life and situations will start to become what we have been asking for, for so long. We are awakened out of a deep sleep and are shown the true essence of life. Why settle for the mundane ways of your past when you can live in the inspiration of the present and future? We throw away the old personality that we once knew ourselves to be and re-clothe ourselves in this cutting-edge, life-on-the-forefront-of-creation personality. We become someone who never lets fear stop us from being, doing, or having anything in life. We become someone who makes our own way, regardless of what others think or feel we should be doing. We continue to push forward even though society says it's not possible to achieve such a thing; we know something so different to be true. We believe so fully in miracles that they become everyday occurrences.

Fear or Freedom

*W*hich way will you choose to live? So many of us are held back by fear and doubt that we never get to experience pure joy. We somehow believe that if we go cautiously through life, we will be safe from harm. Fear is a poison that we begin to pollute our children with from the time of conception. We were poisoned with it, and then we pass on that poison. We must stop the insanity of this teaching. Not only do we teach it through our words, but we also teach it through our energy. We project it to our children before they're even able to talk. We worry incessantly about everything they do in life instead of confidently knowing that they're made of the same energy as Source/God. We disable them instead of enable them. Now that we are where we are, and since we cannot change what our parents did to us in childhood, we must make the choice for ourselves regarding how to move forward from here.

Will we hold ourselves back from really living life because of fear, or will we choose freedom? Freedom is at the very core of who we are. It is our innermost thirst and desire. Joy and freedom—with those two things, you're unstoppable. Our non-physical loved ones are living complete freedom and joy in every moment. So whenever we're feeling either of these two emotions, we're lined up with them and are now riding the same wave of energy. This is when we can co-create with them and they can bring their higher level of thinking into our experience. They so enjoy doing this; there are really no words to express the "high" they get from sharing this world with us.

As we become confident in this process, our loved ones become more and more intertwined in *all* that we do, each and every day. Sometimes we have a feeling or sense that they are there and a part of our experience. Sometimes we'll feel them physically, maybe a touch to the back or shoulder, or heat around our hand. Expressing heat around my hand was one of the things my daughter used to do to let me know she was there. Our loved ones are trying to work with us, trying to get our attention. Sometimes we will hear them directly, and sometimes their message will come to us through someone else. They often come through in our dreams because this is when we're in a relaxed state and can more easily allow them in. I say *allow them in* because when our minds are so full of thoughts, then we can't hear them communicating with us. If we go into a light meditation that stops all the thoughts, then we can hear them clearly. They can guide us gently along our path.

The point is that *anytime* we ask for help and guidance, not only do we have them, but we have a huge non-physical staff to help us with all of the answers. Not only will they guide you along, they will make the path for you. It's just a matter of asking and then knowing that it will be so. That's it. Seems too easy, doesn't it? Life is supposed to be easy though. Life is supposed to be fun and cutting-edge, not boring and mundane!

You can start this process by becoming aware of the fears that lie within you. You will be completely blown away by how often fear creeps in. Once you become aware of it, you can make it your business to dissolve that fear. Ask yourself, *What is the purpose of this fear of* _____ *? How is this holding me back from becoming the extraordinary person that I want to be? How is this keeping me in the same, old, mundane life that I have clearly made a choice to become free from?* Then release the fear and give it back to whomever or whatever it came from. Keep repeating this process until you're finally starting to feel that even though a fear may creep up here and there, you're not feeding into it anymore the way you used to.

Now, the next step is to recognize others' fears around you and to refrain from taking them on as your own. You may feel a fear just by being near someone or hearing them talk about it. Recognition is your best tool for combating their projection of fear onto you. This is extremely important on your road to freedom—that you do *not* take on other people's fears! You have to hold firmly to what you know. Despite how much you love and trust someone, do not for any reason go to a place of fear with them. Stay strong in your knowing who you are and what you came to do, and they will become inspired by this. Never meet anyone in their fear. Going there with them will bring you out of your own energy vortex and will not give you the freedom that you are wanting.

Millions of people live in fear each and every day, and the only way to remove yourself from it is to rise above the energy of fear to where our loved ones lovingly reside. Staying in a place of joy and love is a protective force that doesn't allow the insecurities that fear brings into your experience. Those around you will watch as you move through life with ease and excitement. It's the greatest inspiration. It will be almost as if you posses a gift that is so rare and unusual that people will be in awe of this enlightenment. They will wonder how someone who has gone through so much heartache can be so filled with love and appreciation for life. They will look to you, the one who suffered through the pain of loss, and ask, "How do I attain such joy?" You will say to them, "I have a knowing and an understanding of All That Is—a place where there's no such thing as loss, only gain and growth. A place where limitlessness exists. Come to this place with me, and you will see it too!"

Heaven on Earth

*C*an a heavenly quality of life truly be a part of our experience now, here on earth? The answer to this is *yes*. I am proof of this. The only thing that separates us from this heavenly place is our thinking and our conditioning. We have become so conditioned to think that heaven is only a place for those who die, and then only a select few at that. This is so far from the truth. Our close-minded thought patterns are the only things that separate us from the heavenly plane where love and abundance of all things prevails. Lack does not exist in this heavenly place because that is not a part of God, Creator, or Source. Lack is *only* a human-conditioned perception.

We connect to this heavenly place by lining up our energy to it. First, we need to believe in it. If we do not believe that it's possible, it will never become a part of our experience. Period. We must open our mind to this possibility even if we have some reservations or doubts about it. Once you open your mind to this idea, you will then be drawn by a powerful force to heavenly experiences. You will experience the life force that's all around you and in every creation you can see and touch. You will feel the creator's embrace in all that you do and ask for. You will start to believe in something much bigger than you ever have before. This is enlightenment. Your truth will be told by you and through you. Your uncertainties will become certainties. Your fears and doubts will become knowingness and fearlessness. The world will begin to transform before your eyes. Disbelief of the power around you will turn into belief of something so vast and so infinite that you can see no end and no beginning to it. It is the immeasurable, the vortex of creation.

I am so excited for you to start this process because I know of the deliciousness that it will bring to you. Alignment of energy is really what this process is about. It is about rising above the drudgery of this world, knowing that you are being raised to a higher place of awareness and love. Life can be filled with drudgery, or it can be magical. You have the power to decide which life you choose to live.

In all thoughts large and small are your creations of this time-space reality. It is a choosing that you do each and every day. No more excuses that life is out of your control. It is far more in your control than you have ever thought to be possible. When someone has lost someone dear to them, the pain is an opportunity to fully embrace the emotions this life can bring to you. This has now become an amazing opportunity for you to go within and know that you are being called to this heavenly place, which is awaiting you with unconditional love and every belief in the power that you possess! If we could all get to this place at least once, we would never question the powers that create worlds and the powers of unconditional love.

Heaven knows no fear, only love. This is where all power lies. Those who rule with fear have no true power. They are disconnected from who they truly are and will fall away from your life experience when you're connected in this heavenly love. Try this and you'll see the power you have as you stay connected to this place of love and limitlessness while the other person is in a place of fear. They will falter without the power that is connected to All That Is. They will become unsteady in purpose or action while you stand firm with faith and a knowledge of the power you have within you to create your own experiences.

Most religions teach fear, yet at the same time they teach faith. Faith is a belief not based on proof but on trust in the truth or worthiness of something unseen. If you truly have this faith, you would not act from a place of fear. You would know that you don't have to worry about things around you going wrong because you would have faith that all things are made right for you. This is something we must remind ourselves of because we are constantly bombarded with fear from others. Lift yourself above the fears of others, and they will be inspired by your faith and your knowledge that love and joy abound. Joy is the state of well-being, a state of happiness and bliss. Faith is when something wanted does not work out for you, and you continue to trust that a better situation is awaiting you.

Faith is knowing that all things large and small are being tended to by those in this heavenly place. When you raise your energy to this heavenly place, you can feel all of these things working for you.

It's as if everything is in a perfect flow and life just falls right into place. It is not until we leave this energy alignment that we tend to feel awkward and out of balance. We tend to lose our trust and faith in *all* things working out for us.

You must decide how important it is for you to continually lift your energy to this heavenly place even when situations around you cause you to lose your footing. The times when we leave are our times to experience contrast. This contrast will help us to know fully what it is that we want and don't want. Often, we curse at the contrast, but without it, we would never know where we want to go from here. We would just stay idle. There is no stopping or standing if you want your life to feel good. Energy is always moving, and if we do not keep up with this moving energy, we cannot participate in this heavenly experience.

This heaven I speak of is a part of a constantly moving energy. It is *always* in a state of creation. Creation is the act of making, inventing, or producing. Creation is the act of bringing the world into ordered existence. This has not stopped; it is a continual flow of energy that will always be. When you connect to this heavenly place, you will feel the energy moving quickly. The more you've experienced through contrast, the more asking you have done. The more asking you have done, the faster this stream of energy will be moving. For instance, in my previous marriage, I was not appreciated and it was very sad to feel that way. No matter what I did, it was never right. That experience caused to me to live a contrast because it felt bad. In that contrast, I did a lot of asking to be loved and appreciated. In ALL of that huge amount of asking, the energy revolved around that subject began to move very fast.

Until I got myself out of the situation that felt so bad, I would not be able to feel good or allow the universe to bring to me the relationship that would answer this huge asking. Once I got out of it, I allowed the answer to my asking into my life. The answer was the husband I have now, who has a HUGE amount of appreciation for me! I wouldn't recommend becoming stuck in any situation that leads to such a huge amount of asking because it feels like trying to stop traffic with your body. It is *only* your thinking that makes you *feel stuck* in any situation in your life. There are always solutions; you just have to open your mind to them.

The mind is your most powerful tool of creation. The body simply follows the mind. That's why so many of us are sick or ill; it is due to our mind's resistant thoughts. Many will tell you to meditate, to stop negative thoughts. When you stop negative thoughts, you stop negatively creating in your life and body. What thoughts will you choose instead?

Choosing a Thought

How many of us have grown accustom to choosing the negative thought over the positive one? We have been conditioned to this negative thinking from previous generations. When do we stop the insanity of this? When do we start teaching the new generations coming in that our thoughts have everything to do with our life experiences and if you want to live a healthy, wonderful life, free of sickness and misery, you must change your thinking? When do we start teaching them what powerful creators they are and how to become aware of this heavenly place that we all have access to?

We can begin doing things now, in a new way, so that our children do not have to wait decades to tap into this well-being. The fact of the matter is, we are all born with this knowing but have been forced and conditioned into believing something quite different. We have disabled our children instead of enabling them. We teach them fear from day one of their life here. If we are not directly teaching them, we are energetically teaching them. They feel every emotion we have around them from the time of conception.

If we are all given the choice of thought, then why would we ever choose a negative one? It is most often what we do automatically. It is only by being aware of these negative thoughts that we can choose a softer way of viewing life situations. These brainwave patterns are so used to sending a thought into a negative direction that we must retrain them. When you catch yourself thinking a negative thought, remind yourself that this was an old way of thinking and you are creating a new pattern of thinking. Then you can redirect *any* negative thought pattern into one that is positive. For instance, if you think, *I will never have a job that I love; I hate this job, and my life is miserable,* you have just signed yourself on for that very experience. Instead, you can start off by saying, *My job hasn't been the best, but it is only temporary. I know that my possibilities are endless and I am looking forward to seeing what can come my way.* You have gone from closing the door to your better life to opening it with just those few little words.

Those of us who have lost a loved one (physically speaking) have a huge opportunity to turn something seemingly horrible into a magnificent miracle. My hope is that by the end of this book, you will have experienced the enlightenment that can help you to turn your loss into a positive situation—that you will find yourself in a place of appreciation for how it was able to open your eyes to living life a different way. That you will find yourself in true appreciation for this physical life experience, be it long or short, allowing each day to present miracles to you. Rather than living life as drudgery and thinking *why me*, you will live life for all the fabulous opportunities coming your way.

If choosing a thought is all you have to do to begin to live life in amazement, then what could possibly stop you? This is not hard. No one has asked you to move mountains or climb Mt. Everest (though some do.) This is *all* about something you have complete and total control over—choosing your thoughts. Simple. Almost too simple. Isn't it wonderful to know that it was so well thought out and that no other can create for you? That you don't have to battle the world to get the life experience you want, you just have to change your waves of thinking? My new life story can be, *I was broken into pieces and I was angry about how life can be so cruel, but I realized that so many positive things came from this situation. I can now share my story of inspiration with others and help them to heal. The possibilities for a better life now are endless and I am really excited to see this information inspire others to live life with greatness.* Get yourself to this heavenly place and watch life unfold with such ease that you will then ask, *how in the world have I missed out on this for all these years?*

Establishing the New You

We sometimes have wonderful intentions of making a full life change, and then we remember that we have very resistant people around us in our life—people who will not be open to such a huge life change. This is an important part to read if you're faced with any adversities within your family, friends, or job.

It's critical for you to remember this: *one person who is connected and fearless is more powerful than a million who are not.* Those who are coming at you with any kind of resistance are *not* connected to well-being! Period. I am promising that if you stay grounded in your *new way*, they will become inspired by *you*. This is an amazing opportunity to not only help yourself but all of those whom you love and care about in your life. Depending on how far along you are in your growth and strength, this can sometimes be an ongoing process, for a while at least.

Those who love and care about you may be so convinced that you're not capable of making clear and wise decisions that they will bombard you with *their* fears. Go into it knowing that you will rise above this fear-based energy. Remember that they are projecting *their* fears and not yours! Family members often think that since they love you so much they are looking out for your best interest. So they tell you to be careful in everything you do, as if you don't have the power and wisdom within you to make the right decisions. They continually go to the old-fashion way of disabling those around them instead of enabling. You will politely remind them that they should trust in you, just as you trust in yourself. You will explain that you are going on with life, from this point forward, to live and enjoy it fully, without fear holding you back. This will become less and less of an issue as you become fully confident with this shift. They will begin to leave you alone and let you be. They will see that they no longer need to guide and direct you because life for you is getting really, really good! Then once it starts to get *really* good, they will become inspired by *you*. They will begin to watch you and want those same experiences that just pop up left and right for you! Then you will say to them that you dropped all the fear and worry and picked up *belief and knowing*, and now look at what begins to unfold. You will allow them to see creation unfold right before their very eyes. Then you have inspired through your own life experience. Beautiful!

Clearing Out

As this beautiful shift takes place, you're likely to have the desire to lighten the load in your home and surroundings. This will mean de-cluttering your space. With every item you remove, you have also removed the energy attached to that piece. When you think about it, we have closets that are cluttered, drawers that are cluttered, basements that are cluttered, and so many other things. Go to your refrigerator and see how much stuff is in there that you haven't used in years! It's amazing to think about all these different areas that collect so much clutter on a daily basis. Begin today to remove the old from *one* area and see how good it feels. This will inspire you to go room by room and do the same thing throughout your entire home, car, and office. There is much to be said for a clean and organized house. After all, cleanliness is godliness.

If we want to partake in this lighter heavenly energy, then we must remove the old ways of our past. Buy only those things you need and will use, and in doing this, you will avoid rebuilding the clutter and collection of heavy energy throughout your home.

Remember this is all a part of rebuilding your life a different way, one that works, and not only works but is everything you always wanted it to be.

This next topic may be a little harder to wrap your head around, but we're on the subject of clearing out and this is also a part of it. This leads me to *relationships* that you may have in your life. Now would be the time to reevaluate how well they are serving the *new you* and if they are going to be holding you back in any way. For instance, if you have friends that are very nice but do not have any evidence of evolving, then you may want to rethink these friendships. It may not be necessary to shut them out completely, but you may find yourself gently moving on to other things they will not fit in with. The powers that be do this naturally for you—they remove these non-energy matches—but it's important for you not to resist this shift. You must allow them to fall by the wayside as you press forward. Sometimes it's hard to do this, especially if the relationship is one that served you well in the past, yet now it's not and you can't figure out why or how the change happened. I'm going to tell you how it happened. You are now working from a different platform of energy; you have outgrown them. When you try to match yourself to where they are, you will feel the misalignment that holds you two apart. You must hold yourself in your new platform if you want to feel good. If you try to go to where they are, you will feel negative emotions. One of two things will happen; either they will come up to speed with where you now stand, or they will stay where they are and not get where you are going. With our without them, you are moving with the energy that creates worlds, and that is so cool and exciting!

Buckle Up

When you have tapped into this flow of well-being, the energy moves very fast! Once you have taken on this new, lighter energy, you will see how fast your life shifts. There will be a tipping point, and once you hit that, it will catapult you into a whole new life situation. You may experience a job shift, a move, or even a relationship change. It may sound scary (fear-based) at first, but you will soon feel so released from this dense energy that you have carried for so long that it will feel enlightening to come to a place that feels so much better to you. After just a few weeks, you may have gone through so much transformation that friends you haven't seen in that time will be amazed by the sudden clarity of your direction in life.

With a lighter energy and a clearer road ahead, hold onto your pants because this is when life gets really, really good! I remember when I came back from an Abraham-Hicks well-being (life is suppose to be fun) cruise and so much had happened on this trip that those around me were shocked with all of my updates. This is when I discovered that I would be starting a company with Nancy and I would begin writing books immediately. It all felt so right. We knew that as this new idea was spoken through our mouths, it was creation working through us! That is magical! We didn't need confirmation from anyone else that we should be doing this because we knew that it was already in the works. We knew that our non-physical staff was already lining this up for us, and not only lining it up but helping us every step of the way as we began to build this new company. It was heaven working through us to create something that would inspire the world with our ability to tell our stories through our books. We would be connected with everyone we needed to be in order to make this a success, and the co-creators would be brought to us that needed to be a part of this bigger message. The ideas and concepts flow effortlessly through us to keep us at the leading edge of today's business world. Where else can you find better guidance and direction but from those on this heavenly plane of energy? Who knows it better than they do? They are Source energy!

What is about to happen to you will happen so quickly that it'll feel almost as if you need to buckle up your seatbelt of life! The ways of your past and things taking years to manifest for you are no longer part of your experience. Let's just say that within one year, your life could have drastic changes in it—changes so profound that even you are amazed by such a transformation. For some of you, the thought of this may be scary and exciting all at the same time. Know that as these things start to work themselves into your life experience, they will feel like the next logical step. You will sometimes see that something is about to happen and you're not quite sure how or when it will be, but there is a deep inner knowing that it *is* coming. Make sure you don't try to force this to happen, because if there's one thing you must realize, it's that by forcing something you are actually resisting it from coming. You put yourself in a place of non-allowing, which will put a halt on things coming through. The how's and the when's are not our work. Plain and simple. This is the work of our very powerful and all-knowing, non-physical staff. They are behind the scenes lining all of these things up for you in ways that are better then you could have even asked for! That is so cool and so exciting and so *easy*! Remember that life is supposed to be easy and enjoyable—and not drudgery like we have all been taught.

Maybe you a have caught onto the idea by now that up till now your life has been a mere fraction of the greatness it could have been. These old ways will no longer suit you now that you have enjoyed the lightness and the speed of this new energy that you have come to know and love.

Your New Life Story

*I*t's fascinating to realize that your life is changing direction, and not only is it changing direction, but you have the creative tool to begin life a new way. That tool is your mind. The powerful mind that we have been given sets us apart from all other living things on this planet. We have not even touched the surface of what our minds are capable of, and that's pretty amazing. We have so much more to discover within our thinking mechanism that it is almost untouched. Think about this ... if we are only using a fraction of our brain at this time, then what are our capabilities when we begin to use more and more of it? The only thing that holds us back from anything in life is our thinking.

What if we made it our business to begin to ask our minds to open up to greater and greater possibilities? What if you said to your brain that you wanted to use more of it, and then you got out of the way and allowed it to happen? You would become a super genius creator! The more open your mind is, the more creative force you are allowing to flow through it. This very powerful creative force is a part of All That Is and is now flowing through you for endless possibilities.

As we begin to tell our new life story with all of this in mind, we have accessed a very powerful force that can bring to you *all* that you have ever wanted. So from this day forward, if you don't want it, *don't tell it*! If you're not happy with the relationship you have with your parents and you tell this story every day of how you don't have a good relationship with your parents, then your life experience will continue to reflect this same relationship. You must stop telling the same story. Your words are a very powerful part of your creating. Stop and think before you speak. Ask yourself, *is this what I want to continue to be a part of my life or do I want something different?* If you want something different, begin to tell something different. For example: *It's never too late to change how we do things in life, and it would be great to find the things that my parents and I have in common and then build off of those things! I would love for us to have great conversations about our vacations and how much we enjoy traveling.* This could be a good place to start, something believable and without resistance to the subject at hand. You take what part is working or a common ground and you expand on that part. Then leave out the rest (the negative.) This new life story should consist of things from the largest detail to the smallest detail and everything in between.

Life will show you what you are wanting out of it through the contrast that you are living. When you feel depressed, you will need to tell the happy story. Then when you begin to tell the story, tell it with all of the details of how you would like it to be. Make your life story as happy as you want it to be. Get into it, have fun with it. It may feel goofy at first, but it's actually really fun once you begin to get into the nitty-gritty of it all. At first, it may sound like a lie, but it's not because you've already done an asking for it on some level.

You have asked through your contrast, and when you ask, it is always given to you. Where is it then if I'm not living it? It is being held in your powerful escrow or management account. Anything you have ever asked for is lovingly awaiting you. Think of your non-physical staff as your managers. They have opened an account for you at the Bank of Universal Forces. Every time you ask for anything that contrast brings you to know that you want, they make a magnificent deposit to your account. This has been happening since the day you entered this physical life, so think about *all* of the wonderful things that you have amassing in this account. Of course as you bump along, what you have put in there may grow bigger and culminate different facets, as to the magnitude of your asking. For example, when you suffer a really hard hit in life, you often do a *huge* asking for life to not hurt so much and for it to be so much better than what you are going through. You say, "This hurts so bad that I want to die from the pain I feel," and in those moments of hurting, you have done a huge asking for life to be greater than great! To be beyond fantastic in every way! So now the deposit was made (in your pain of your loss, you asked). Once you have done this asking (even viscerally), the answers to this are starting to line up in perfect order for you to enjoy. Those way, way, way better things are now being lovingly held for you in this account with the Bank of Universal Forces, and as soon as you can begin to open up to allowing it in (you allow it in partly by being in a state of appreciation for life and all that you have just lived), they begin to flood into your life experience in immeasurable ways! The way you will begin to allow these things in is to start telling the story of what you have in your account. Did you hear that? I really want you to hear it. *The way you begin allowing these things in is by starting to tell the story of what is in your account (with the Bank of Universal Forces).* Most of us have so much already built up in there that we can begin getting one return after another after another.

Now, this means that all of you who have been given a "bad" deal in life not once, not twice, but many, many times over will benefit the most from the Bank of Universal Forces. You are the ones who have done more asking than others. So what happens? Your account gets bigger and bigger and bigger. This is not to say that you must suffer to be given a return in life. Everyone here has lived contrast, and in every contrast you have an asking. There are undoubtedly those who have not seen tragedy and yet have had a huge asking or desire for more, and this can be given to *anyone* that asks and *allows.* This book is geared toward those who have suffered loss and to ALL of you who have known of this: you have not suffered in vein. There are huge blessings awaiting you. You have so many blessings that if someone were to give you a sneak preview of your account, you would be literally blown away with the mountains of experiences, life changes, money, qualities, and many, many other things that are in there!

So, if I were you, I would begin right now telling your story the way you want it to be and never again tell it the way you don't! Really have fun with this process because life is meant to be fun in every way. This life is meant to be your playground. Get into it, have fun with it, play like you did when you were a kid on the playground. It didn't matter what was happening the next day or the next hour for that matter. You were living so much in your present moment that you were fully experiencing life! Open up the door, see life as you have asked for it to be, and peek in on this powerful account that you have created in the contrast that life brought to you.

Finding Good in Everything

We are all given the choice to think the thoughts we want to think. With the free choice comes the ability to turn every situation in your life experience into one that has benefit and value—not only value, but a life-changing quality. As I have mentioned before, those of us who have gone through what we call "traumatic" or "horrible" experiences, have a huge savings account amassed in the Bank of Universal Forces. In every contrast that makes us ask for something else, it has been fully deposited into our account. Now we need to choose to get on board with the receiving end of it. This is where our free choice of thought comes in. We always, in every situation, have the ability to see good in our life experiences. From the big things to the small things, there is always a *thought choice*. Sometimes we have chosen a "why me" approach, but when we do that, we are hugely missing the gift coming out of this situation. Someone may say, "What good can come out of losing a child? How could anyone turn that into something good?" From the surface, the situation seems completely awful and unfair, but I promise you that if you're open to allowing the gift to come to you, it will. If you open yourself up and say, "I don't have to feel the way I feel forever, and as every day goes by, I heal, and as I heal, I *allow* this gift to come forth and show me how to live happily through this tragedy, not only happily but with *purpose.*"

You see, losing my daughter (physically speaking) gave my life a purpose that it never had before. Yes, it broke me to smithereens for a few months, and then as I lifted here and there from the hurt and the hit of this loss, I began to ask for the deeper purpose in all of this. Eventually I started to open my mind to how this was a gift that was given. I had a choice. Was I going to blame God or take the gift that was being offered to me? This experience gave me so much—everything offered in this book and even more. There will be times that finding the gift will not interest you at all, but when the darkness pulls away for even a short time, reflect in that moment as to what was lovingly given to you through this experience—even if all you come out of it with is to live life, and I mean really *live it.* Enjoy everything and all of those around you by living in a place of appreciation for having them for whatever time you do. Stop sweating the small stuff because none of it matters anyway. When you worry about something, it doesn't change anything! So stop, and just live. Enjoy and savor all of creation and those who are in your life for this moment. Know that life is a great gift and you will enjoy it for as long as you have it here and beyond.

Heartache and pain allow us the opportunity to go within and see the miracles in our life. They are a wakeup call, so to speak, for a life change so huge that it will bring you to this place of enlightenment. Enlightenment is *a final blessed state free from ignorance, desire, and suffering.* You are no longer held in bondage by suffering. You have become awakened to life as it is in the heavenly realm, where all things are possible and attainable. Fear and lack are perceptions of this world and are part of an illusion. When life throws you lemons and you wanted oranges, you know that this is all a part of a bigger plan. All of these hurts lift you to a higher ground when you understand this learning curve. You may not have the power to change what *is*, but you certainly have the power to change your thinking on what *is*.

Things are not as out of control as we may think when we understand that we have the power to change thought. When something happens to us that beats us down, we can always turn our mind and thought into seeing that there's a light for us in our not so far future. I can tell you from my own experience that when I lost my daughter it took me a few months to begin to live life again. Once I started to get myself back on track, our dog (and best friend), Maia, got hit by a car and we almost lost her too. It's not always easy to believe that better days are ahead after going through those things, but something inside me told me to just hold tight and have faith in the unseen. I likened Maia's accident to my life; she took a hit so hard she almost died, and it took her months to get well again. The impact of losing my daughter hit me so hard I thought I might die from the pain. However, these situations made both Maia and me stronger in the end. Every day, we live with a deep appreciation of what gifts we have been given. She is more than happy to stay in our yard and sniff around in complete enjoyment that she is still here and feeling so much better. She's decided to slow down and appreciate what's around her instead of trying to run toward something that she wants. She stays in a place of allowing what's going to come to her to arrive whenever it's presented to her. She, even being a dog, learned enlightenment from her own trauma. We can all learn and grow each and every day, and each and every new experience we have can bring growth.

Appreciation Brings Bliss

*B*liss is a state of profound spiritual satisfaction, happiness, and joy. It is also the state of mind that is undisturbed by gain or loss. Appreciation is a positive emotion or gratitude for something around you. When we show gratitude, we *feel good* and can sense the positive emotion connected to this state of mind. This is a place of being connected to All That Is. This emotion directly connects you to our Source or God. This is the greatness of the heavenly realm. Those that are a part of this heavenly realm are always in a place of appreciation and a state of bliss. When we mirror these emotions, we too are swept into this heavenly realm along with them and All That Is. Appreciation is something that is easy to do and brings a *huge* return.

You always feel good, positive emotions when you're in a place of appreciation—every time, without exception. If you make a mental list of all the things that you have appreciation for, from the time you wake in the morning until the time you sleep at night, you will begin to see evidence of things to be grateful for very quickly, and even more positive things coming to you. What you are saying by appreciating is *yes, more of these things please!* It is your attitude of gratitude that lets your powerful non-physical staff know that you are wanting more and more of these good things.

It is in this power of positive appreciation that we again line up with the energy of our loved ones who are no longer in their human form. Now we can feel them and hear them and know that they are very much still living—and not only are they living, they are thriving. So here is the beautiful part: you can thrive too when you connect to this energy that they are now residing in forevermore! That is so very much a part of the gift that comes with the physical loss of a child or loved one. There are so many different ways to get to them and co-create with them, be it through appreciation, love, joy, meditation, or just opening your mind and not creating resistant thought. Any of these vehicles of emotion will take you to the energy of source. When your non-physical staff sees your appreciation and delivers something wonderful to you, continue to stay in a place of gratitude and this continual cycle will reward you over and over and over again.

In every situation, good or bad, we can be appreciative for the "something" that will come out of it, and that is where our "choosing of thought" comes into play. If we continue to show gratitude for a situation that is not very pleasing to us, knowing that this is how the process goes sometimes, then we will reap the heavenly rewards of our positive state of mind. Know that just around the corner is something great and beyond your expectations!

The Gift

I hope that by this point you have discovered some of the many good things that can come out of the experience of losing a child. I wish for you to experience this amazing gift of a *new* life that can be born from this tragic situation. As for the pain, it will never fully leave you, but the new point of asking that it has brought you to can make life so much more special then it could ever have been before this. I always have this feeling of *what's next?* I wonder what great things are in store for me while not forgetting to enjoy this moment and what is right now. I try to live in this moment and feel the enjoyment of life fully. We can do this alongside the ones we lost. We can *feel* the essence of them and how amazingly and *fully* they are living life now; we can be a part of the very same energy.

They will show us and guide us whenever we need them. They are always there and always watching to see how they can make you see that life is supposed to be good and fun! They want so much for what happened to be an awakening so that we never live life in the same way again. The next time you eat something delicious, know that they are eating it with you and enjoying it beyond words. The next time you smell a flower, know that they are smelling it with you and it's intoxicating. The next time someone you love gives you a hug, they are feeling such unconditional love for that embrace. They are laughing with you and vacationing with you and experiencing all of these things with you. Remember there is no age to a soul; the loved one you lost (physically) is fully aware of *all* things.

Our loved ones have given us a gift of becoming what we truly came here to be but had forgotten because we were taught something so different. They came here (even for a short time) to remind us. Sometimes we have to experience deep pain in order to *hear* things. They gifted you a different life … one filled with greatness and the presence of their love. *It's a love that will never leave you. It is there for you unconditionally and forevermore. That is beautiful … Norah Lee, thank you for our gift!*

Of the many gifts that we were given was being blessed with the daughter we had so longed to have. One year after losing Norah Lee, our new Angel, Eden May was born full term, full of life and wellbeing! My appreciation for her is rooted so deep that each and every moment with her is filled with more and more blessings.

In memory of Norah Lee

If I could speak to you now~

I would tell you to live life like it's your playground....

I would tell you to love each other more and criticize less....

I would tell you to appreciate each and everything you can and don't let a day go by without being thankful...

I would make sure those around me knew I loved them because I am LOVE....

I would say let all the petty things in life stay far from your mind...because they don't matter...

I would say when you give love...you get it back...so when you leave here my one wish is to send you on your way with love......

Dedication

To my Husband, Patrick, for giving me two beautiful daughters that have changed my life and have inspired me to live life to the fullest.

To my Boys~ Devon, Tiernan and Calen. You are the men who grew me into a wonderful Mother.

Acknowledgements

My greatest teachers, Abraham-Hicks. There are no teachers on earth today that offer such unconditional love and leading-edge thinking as these wonderful co-creators. Being a part of their Well-Being Cruise, just a couple of months after my loss, was the most profound lift that enabled me to write this book.

To Amy and Colleen, who took care of me when I lost the will to do it for myself. I love you both so very much. I consider myself very blessed to have two friends as wonderful as both of you!

Nancy Burke, author of: *From We to Me*. Your book and suggestions gave me the hope and belief that I needed to connect with Our Love, Norah Lee.

Michael Bang. You held so strong to the knowing that she was not gone and death is not what everyone fears it to be. You knew and believed she would come back to us, and *she did*!

Daryl Ponder, my neighbor and friend. Thank you so much for all of your love, support and expertise in the English Language.

To my editor, Elizabeth Day. You are amazing! I love that the Universe brought us together. Thank you for your belief in this message. You inspired me to move forward, and for that I am eternally grateful.